Thurgood Marshall

FIGHT FOR JUSTICE

Thurgood Marshall
FIGHT FOR JUSTICE

by Rae Bains
illustrated by Gershom Griffith

Troll Associates

Library of Congress Cataloging-in-Publication Data

Bains, Rae.
  Thurgood Marshall: fight for justice / by Rae Bains; illustrated
by Gershom Griffith.
      p.   cm.
  Summary: Examines the life of the first Afro-American to be
appointed to the Supreme Court.
  ISBN 0-8167-2827-5 (lib. bdg.)   ISBN 0-8167-2828-3 (pbk.)
  1. Marshall, Thurgood, 1908-   —Juvenile literature.   2. United
States. Supreme Court—Biography—Juvenile literature.   3. Judges—
United States—Biography—Juvenile literature.   4. Civil rights—
United States—History—Juvenile literature.   [1. Marshall,
Thurgood, 1908-   .   2. United States.   Supreme Court—Biography.
3. Judges.   4. Afro-Americans—Biography.]   I. Griffith, Gershom,
ill.   II. Title.   III. Title: Fight for justice.
KF8745.M34B3   1993
347.73 '2634—dc20
[B]
[347.3073534]
[B]   92-37302

This edition published in 2001.

Thurgood Marshall

FIGHT FOR JUSTICE

"Thurgood, since you won't sit still and let your classmates do their work, take yourself to the principal's office!"

The other boys and girls giggled. Nine-year-old Thurgood Marshall pretended he didn't care as he walked slowly from the room. But he did care. He knew the punishment that was coming. He would have to stay after school and learn another part of the Constitution of the United States. That was what the principal made him do every time he acted up in class.

Another after-school ball game missed, Thurgood thought gloomily. Another hour in that hall outside the principal's office. Another page of long, hard words to learn by heart. Worst of all, another long, hard lecture at home. There was no way to hide his punishment from his parents. Mama was a teacher in the Division Street school, and she'd *know*!

Thurgood got into trouble so often, he had memorized all of the Constitution except for some of the amendments at the end. And little by little, he was working his way through those. This afternoon his assignment was the Fourteenth Amendment.

The boy read the first part of the amendment. He read it again, out loud. He thought about the words he was saying. They seemed very important.

That night, at dinner, Thurgood sat quietly
through his parents' lecture. Finally, he said,
"I'm sorry." Then he asked about something
that had been on his mind since that afternoon.
"What does the Fourteenth Amendment mean
when it says that a state can't deny anybody
'the equal protection of the laws'? Doesn't that
mean the laws should be equal for Negroes and
white people? So why can't I sit anywhere I
want to at the ballpark? Or on the trolley car?"

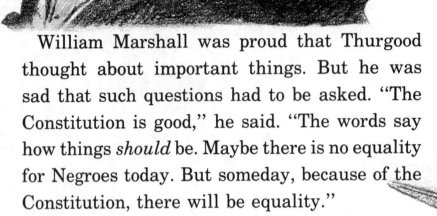

William Marshall was proud that Thurgood thought about important things. But he was sad that such questions had to be asked. "The Constitution is good," he said. "The words say how things *should* be. Maybe there is no equality for Negroes today. But someday, because of the Constitution, there will be equality."

"The Constitution is a guide," Norma Marshall said. "It's like a rule book for Americans. The country doesn't always follow the rules, but they are there. And as your father said, someday...."

Thurgood enjoyed the talks at the dinner table. His parents were smart and fair. And they worked so hard—Mama at teaching, Papa as chief steward of a big country club. The Marshalls were respected members of their Baltimore, Maryland, community.

Norma and William Marshall had high hopes for their sons. They decided that William Aubrey, born in 1904, was going to be a doctor. Thoroughgood, born on July 2, 1908, and named after his Grandpa Marshall, was going to be a dentist. In those days, many white doctors and dentists did not treat black people. There was a real need in the black community for well-trained professionals. The Marshalls wanted their sons to help meet that need.

The Marshall family lived in a pleasant, middle-class neighborhood in West Baltimore. Black children and white children played together on the street in front of their houses. But they went to separate schools.

While he was growing up, young Thurgood (he shortened his name when he was in second grade) saw segregation every day of his life. But it didn't make him feel like a second-class citizen. That was because his parents taught him he was as good as anyone. If he was honest and fair and worked hard, he was anyone's equal—no matter what the law said.

As a teenager, Thurgood still planned to become a dentist. But, thanks to his father, he became more interested in the legal system. Mr. Marshall liked to go to the courthouse and listen to the cases being tried. Whenever possible, Thurgood went with him. They often discussed the trials and verdicts at dinner time. "My father never told me to become a lawyer," Thurgood Marshall said later, "but he turned me into one. He did it by teaching me to argue, by challenging my logic on every point, by making me prove every statement I made."

Thurgood Marshall was proud of his father. One reason was that William Marshall was the first black person to serve on a Baltimore grand jury. A grand jury listens to all the facts when someone is charged with a crime. Then it decides if there is enough evidence to put the accused person on trial.

The first time Mr. Marshall was a grand juror, something bothered him. He noticed that his fellow jurors always asked if the accused person was black or white. He also noticed that black people were more often sent to trial than white people. If the accused person was white, the case was often dismissed.

Mr. Marshall objected to this. He said it was wrong to ask a person's color before deciding if there was a case against that person. The other grand jurors said nothing. They were shocked that a black man had the nerve to object to the system. Then the foreman of the grand jury made a ruling. The question of race was not to be asked again.

This example of his father's courage filled young Thurgood with admiration. It also showed how important it was for black people to become involved in the legal system. It was clear that blacks had to speak up for their rights if they wanted justice and equality.

The Times

SEPTEMBER 13, 1922

Negro Man Speaks Out

William Marshall, the first negro to serve on a grand Jury in Baltimore, objected

to his fellow jurors asking the color of the accused, before making a decision about a case.

When Thurgood graduated from high school in
1925, he followed his brother, Aubrey, to Lincoln
University. Lincoln was a small school in
Pennsylvania. It had about 300 students, all
black men, and an all-white teaching staff. The
standards were high and the courses were
difficult. Aubrey Marshall did very well at
Lincoln. After graduation, he went to medical
school and became a highly respected surgeon.

19

At Lincoln, Thurgood did enough studying to earn a B average. But he didn't spend all his time with books. There were sports, the debating team, pep rallies, parties, dances, and fraternity activities.

In Thurgood Marshall's second year at Lincoln, he got into trouble for taking part in a fraternity prank. The school suspended him and his friends. Marshall did a lot of thinking. He thought about his parents saving their money for his college costs. He thought about the summer months and after-school hours he had worked to pay some of his school bills. He had worked as a grocery clerk, baker, waiter, delivery boy, and bellhop. Getting thrown out of school for fooling around was childish, he realized. Marshall decided it was time to grow up.

When he returned to Lincoln, the "new" Marshall threw himself into serious studying. He read the works of black novelists, poets, and scholars. Their ideas led him to take a closer look at the life of blacks in America. Marshall and his college friends wanted to be successful, to earn a good income, and to win respect in society. But they also saw their responsibility. They had to do something for blacks who did not have the same chance to go to college as they did.

Racial discrimination weighed heavily on every black American. In the South, the laws kept blacks from enjoying equal rights. And even though there were no segregation laws in the North, blacks did not enjoy equal treatment there.

Right near Lincoln University there was a segregated movie theater. Local custom said that blacks weren't allowed to sit downstairs. They had to sit in the balcony. One night Thurgood Marshall and a group of his friends decided to challenge this custom. They went to the theater and sat in the "whites only" orchestra seats.

COLORED
BALCONY

An usher told the young men to go upstairs. Marshall said, "I paid for my ticket and I'm going to stay where I am." Marshall and his friends watched the movie with everyone else. "The amazing thing was," he wrote to his parents, "when we were leaving we just walked out with those other people and they didn't do anything, didn't say a thing, didn't even look at us—at least, as far as I know. I'm not sure I like being invisible, but maybe it's better than being put to shame and not able to respect yourself."

At the beginning of Marshall's third year of
college, he met Vivian Burey, a senior at the
University of Pennsylvania. Vivian was called
"Buster" by her friends. Thurgood and Buster
met at Cherry Street Memorial Church, fell in
love soon after, and were married in September
1929. Their marriage lasted until Mrs. Marshall
died twenty-six years later.

Thurgood Marshall graduated with honors in June 1930. During his senior year at Lincoln, he had decided not to be a dentist. He wanted to be a lawyer. It was something he had been building toward all his life: learning the Constitution in grammar school; the dinner-time discussions with his parents; the trials he attended with his father; the debating team in college; integrating the local movie theater; reading about the black struggle in America. Marshall was sure that the law was the key to equality for his people.

Marshall applied to the University of Maryland's law school. But because he was black, his application was turned down. So he enrolled in Howard University's law school in Washington, D.C. Howard was founded in 1867 to educate former slaves. Since that time, thousands of black doctors, dentists, lawyers, and other professionals have graduated from Howard.

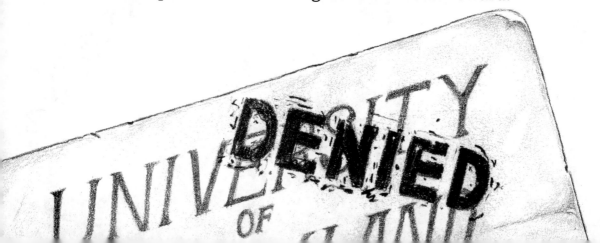

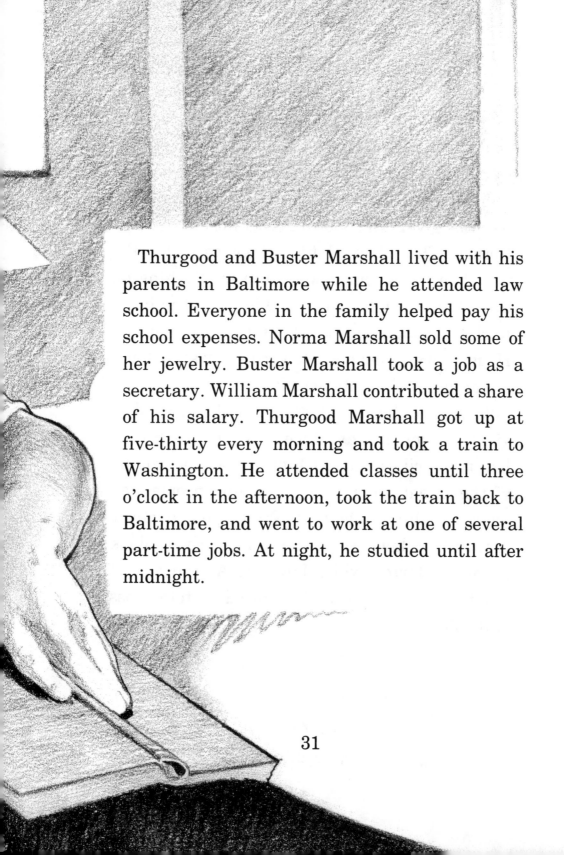

Thurgood and Buster Marshall lived with his parents in Baltimore while he attended law school. Everyone in the family helped pay his school expenses. Norma Marshall sold some of her jewelry. Buster Marshall took a job as a secretary. William Marshall contributed a share of his salary. Thurgood Marshall got up at five-thirty every morning and took a train to Washington. He attended classes until three o'clock in the afternoon, took the train back to Baltimore, and went to work at one of several part-time jobs. At night, he studied until after midnight.

The work and school schedule was so hard that the 6′ 2″ tall student went from 170 pounds to 130. But he finished his freshman year first in his class. In Marshall's second year at Howard, he was given the job of assistant in the law library. The job paid his school costs for the next two years, but it kept him in Washington until late at night. During this time, the hard-working young man got to know Charles Houston. Houston was a dean at Howard's law school and a leading civil rights activist.

When Marshall graduated from law school in 1933, he opened a law office in Baltimore. But he had two strikes against him. It was the middle of the Great Depression, and few people had money to hire a lawyer. White people never hired black lawyers in those days. Even black people preferred white lawyers. At the end of his first year, Marshall showed a total loss of $1,000.

THURGOOD
MARSHALL
Attorney
at Law

In 1934, guided by Charles Houston, Marshall became the official lawyer for the Baltimore branch of the National Association for the Advancement of Colored People (NAACP). This was the real beginning of his legal career. The next year, Marshall and Houston took on a major civil rights case.

Donald G. Murray was a black Maryland college graduate. Murray had applied to the University of Maryland's law school. Like Marshall, he was turned down because he was black.

Marshall and Houston took the University of Maryland to court. They did not fight the segregation laws directly. Instead, they focused on the "separate but equal" decisions of the U.S. Supreme Court. "Separate but equal" meant that states were allowed to set up separate schools for both races, so long as the schools were equal. Of course, everyone knew that blacks and whites did not get equal educations. But that was hard to prove in court.

There was only one law school in Maryland, so there was no doubt that Murray was denied an equal opportunity for education. The court gave the State of Maryland two choices: admit Donald Murray to the law school, or provide a law school for black Maryland college graduates. Since it was too expensive to open a second law school, the school had to admit Murray to the University of Maryland. It was Thurgood Marshall's first great legal victory. In the courtroom, he showed no emotion when the verdict was read. But as soon as he got outside, he threw his arms around his wife and began to dance.

The Murray case was just the beginning for Marshall. Over the next few years, he chipped away at school segregation. In case after case, in Missouri, in Texas, and all over the South, Marshall and the NAACP challenged segregation laws. Each time, they did it by showing that qualified black students did not have equal opportunity for higher education. Each time, the cases were lost in the lower courts. And each time, the U.S. Supreme Court reversed the decision, giving the final victory to Marshall.

In 1938, Marshall became the NAACP's chief counsel. His headquarters were in New York. But he didn't spend much time there. He traveled around the country, going wherever black Americans needed a strong legal voice.

Marshall was always prepared when he went into court, and his courtroom efforts were brilliant. In his years as NAACP counsel, he won twenty-nine cases before the Supreme Court!

State after state felt the effects of Marshall's legal crusade. Segregation laws took a beating at his hands. But the laws remained on the books. Black people were still segregated. That had to end, Marshall vowed. "The terms 'separate' and 'equal' cannot be used together," he said. "There can be no separate equality."

Marshall and the NAACP Legal Defense Fund decided to challenge school segregation at all levels. They did this in a case that is known as *Brown v. Board of Education.* (The letter *v.* stands for *versus,* the Latin word for "against.") There were actually five cases presented to the Supreme Court in 1952 as part of *Brown.* These cases came from Delaware, Virginia, Kansas, Washington, D.C., and South Carolina.

In each case, Marshall and his fellow lawyers attacked the very idea of school segregation. It took a year and a half before the Supreme Court handed down its decision. In May 1954, the highest court in the land declared that school segregation was against the law. "Separate but equal" was not acceptable anymore. Thurgood Marshall was "so happy, I was numb."

But it was only half a victory. A year later, the Supreme Court ruled that the states had to make plans to integrate their schools but did not have to do this right away. The battle was far from over.

Marshall fought segregation on many fronts. There were cases seeking equal rights for blacks in public housing, public parks, sports arenas, and public transportation. Marshall and his fellow lawyers went after every law that discriminated against black people or any other minority.

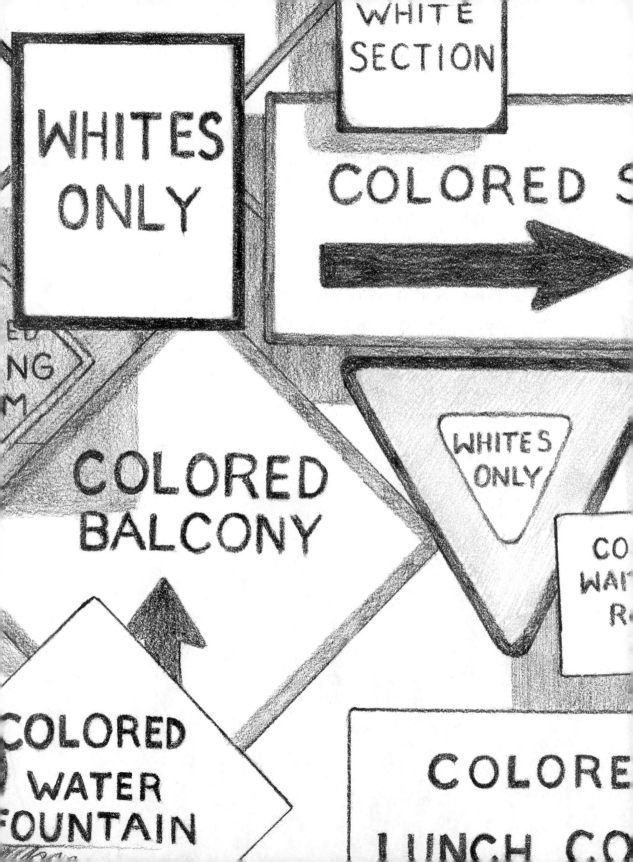

In 1961, Thurgood Marshall was appointed a judge on the U.S. Court of Appeals. This court is one level below the U.S. Supreme Court. Marshall served as an appeals judge for four years. In 1965, President Lyndon Johnson offered Marshall the job of Solicitor General of the United States. The Solicitor General represents the United States in cases that appear before the Supreme Court. Marshall was proud to accept the position. As Solicitor General, he made sure that the Civil Rights Act of 1964 was obeyed. This was what both President Johnson and Marshall wanted—equal rights for *all* Americans.

In 1967, President Johnson appointed Thurgood Marshall to the Supreme Court of the United States. Johnson said, "I believe it is the right thing to do, the right time to do it, the right man and the right place. I believe he has already earned his place in history, but I think it will be greatly enhanced by his service on the Court."

Thurgood Marshall became the ninety-sixth justice to take the oath, and the first black justice in the 178 years of the Supreme Court's history. It was the start of a distinguished career that lasted until Marshall retired in 1991.

During his years on the Court, Marshall remained a powerful spokesman for equal rights, for the freedoms guaranteed by the Constitution, and for peaceful change. As he said, "It takes no courage to get in the back of a crowd and throw a rock. Rather, it takes courage to stand up on your two feet and look anyone straight in the eye and say, 'I will not be beaten.' I say to you... move, but move within the Constitution, and find new ways of moving nonviolently within the Constitution, bearing in mind that there are many of us in this country who will not let it go down the drain."

After Marshall's retirement, Justice Sandra Day O'Connor, another member of the Supreme Court, spoke about his great influence on the Court and its decisions. "Justice Marshall," she said, "imparted not only his legal knowledge but also his life experiences, pushing and prodding us to respond...to the power of moral truth."

Thurgood Marshall once said, "The true miracle of the Constitution was not its birth but its life." He spent his life defending that belief.

After a long life working for justice, Thurgood
Marshall passed away on January 24, 1993.

INDEX